Song Of The Bells

4

Tribal Dance

A BOY AND HIS PIANO

Twenty-one easy pieces for piano

by

STANFORD KING

CONTENTS

March Of The Merry Men

THIS ONE (MARK EXPLAIN MORE ABOUT SHARPS & FLATS

Sailing

Allegretto *(moderately fast)*

Creepy Rhapsody

A Hike Through The Woods

Western Thriller

Here Come The Pipers!

Halloween Pranks

Off To The Races

Desert Caravan

The Village Band

In A Helicopter

Relay Race

The Old Salt's Tale

The Organ At Twilight

Andante *(slowly)*

Ivan And His Concertina

At The Circus

Giocoso *(with sport)*

D.C. al Fine

The Young Skiers

Grazioso *(with grace)*

Mountain Music

The Harmonica And The Banjo